HANDS-ON HISTORY

AZTECS

DRESS, EAT, WRITE AND PLAY JUST LIKE THE AZTECS

FIONA MACDONALD

QED Publishing

QED

Written by Fiona MacDonald
Editor Felicity Fitchard
Designer Liz Wiffen
Projects made by Veronica Erard

Publisher Steve Evans
Creative Director Zeta Davies
Senior Editor Hannah Ray

Printed and bound in China

Picture credits

Key: T = top, B = bottom, C = centre, L = left, R = right, FC
= front cover

The Art Archive: p4 tl: Government Palace Tiaxcala Mexico/
Dagli Orti; p6 tr: Museo Ciudad Mexico/Dagli Orti; p6 br:
Dagli Orti; p8 tl: Museo Ciudad Mexico/Nicolas Sapieha; p8
br, p14 tr, p18 cl: Museo del Templo Mayor Mexico/Dagli Orti;
p10tr, p28 tr: Biblioteca Nacional Mexico/Dagli Orti; p12 tl:
Mireille Vautier; p12 br; p14 cb: Bibliothéque des Arts Déc-
oratifs Paris/Dagli Orti; p16 tr: Antochiw Collection Mexico/
Mireille Vautier; p16 bl: Museum Für Völker Kunde Vienna/
Dagli Orti; p18 ct; p18 br: Biblioteca Nacional Madrid/Dagli
Orti; p20 tl: Mireille Vautier; p20 br: National Anthropologi-
cal Museum Mexico/Dagli Orti; p22 tl: Mireille Vautier; p24 tl:
Dagli Orti.

Bridgeman Art Library: p11 tr: Mexican School (16th
century)/Museo de America, Madrid, Spain; p23 tr: Mexican
School (20th century)/Archives Charmet, Private Collection;
p26 bl: Spanish School (16th century)/Biblioteca Medicea-Lau-
renziana, Florence, Italy.

Corbis: p26 tr: Bob Krist.

Werner Forman Archive: FC: Biblioteca Universitaria,
Bolognia, Italy; p4 br, p24 br: British Museum, London; p28 bl:
Liverpool Museum, Liverpool.

Words in **bold** are explained
in the glossary on page 30.

Website information is correct at the time
of going to press. However, the publishers
cannot accept liability for any information
or links found on third-party websites.

Before undertaking an activity which
involves eating or the preparation of food,
parents and/or teachers should ensure
that none of the children in their care
are allergic to any of the ingredients.
In a classroom situation, prior written
permission from parents may be required.

CONTENTS

WHO WERE THE AZTECS?

The Aztecs ruled an empire in Mesoamerica, the land between North and South America. Before they grew powerful, around 700 years ago, many different civilizations flourished and built cities in this region, including the **Toltecs** and **Maya**. Each of these peoples had its own laws, skills and traditions, but they also shared many religious beliefs and ways of running their communities. The Aztecs learned from the ideas, knowledge and skills of these earlier peoples, and built a civilization that **dominated** Mesoamerica for almost 200 years.

Aztec man (right) and woman (left) say prayers in front of a holy statue. This picture was painted 500 years after the Aztecs lived, but shows us what they looked like.

Mesoamerica (Central America) is shown in yellow here. Tenochtitlan was the Aztecs' capital city.

MEXICO
GULF OF MEXICO
Tenochtitlan
PACIFIC OCEAN
SOUTH AMERICA

DID YOU KNOW?

THE AZTECS' OWN NAME FOR THEMSELVES WAS THE 'MEXICA'. TODAY, WE STILL USE THIS NAME FOR THEIR HOMELAND, MEXICO.

EARLY BEGINNINGS

At first, the Aztecs were poor, wandering hunters, struggling to survive in the dry desert land of North Mexico. But around 1200 CE they migrated south, to the Central Valley of Mexico. They found water, animals and plants – and other people already living there! The Aztecs were not made welcome.

GAINING POWER

For 100 years, the Aztecs worked for the Valley peoples as soldiers and slaves. Around 1300 CE, they rebelled and seized power. They grew rich and strong, and conquered nearby lands. They forced the people they had conquered to give them tribute (tax), such as food, clothes, gold and treasure.

An Aztec pendant shaped like a two-headed poisonous snake. It is made of turquoise (a semi-precious stone) with carved shells for teeth.

MAKE A TWO-HEADED SERPENT STAMP

Snakes were a symbol of the Aztec god Quetzalcoatl (say Keht-tsal-coh-ah-tl). His name means 'feathered serpent'.

YOU WILL NEED: TWO 7 x 11cm RECTANGLES OF CORRUGATED CARD • PENCIL • TRACING PAPER • CRAFT KNIFE • PVA GLUE • WHITE, GREEN AND BLUE ACRYLIC PAINT • SAUCER • BRUSH OR ROLLER • FINE BRUSH • WHITE PAPER

1 Copy or trace the two-headed snake onto one of the card rectangles. Ask an adult to cut it out with a craft knife.

2 To make your stamp block, glue the snake shape to the other card rectangle. Leave to dry completely.

3 Mix up some turquoise paint. Roll or brush paint evenly over the snake shape on your block.

4 Turn the block over and press down firmly onto white paper. Gently peel off the paper to reveal the snake.

5 Let your stamped snake dry, then add highlights, such as the eyes, with white paint and a fine brush.

▲ You can use your stamp over and over again!

LAKE CITY

By 1325 CE, the Aztecs were powerful enough to build a capital city, Tenochtitlan (say Teh-nosh-teet-lahn). It stood on an island in the middle of a lake and was linked to the shore by four massive **causeways** made from pounded earth. A network of canals ran through the city, and people travelled in small boats along them. Fresh water was carried from nearby mountains into the town by a stone **aqueduct**.

In Aztec legend, the god Huitzilopochtli (say Weet-zeel-oh-posh-tlee) told the Aztecs to build their city where they found an eagle sitting on a cactus, eating a snake.

DID YOU KNOW?
IN NAHUATL (SAY NAH-WA-TL), THE AZTEC LANGUAGE, TENOCHTITLAN MEANS 'CACTUS ROCK'.

CAPITAL CITY

Tenochtitlan grew fast and became one of the largest cities in the world. By 1500 CE, it was home to over 200 000 people. European explorers said it was cleaner and better than many of their own cities. It was made up of four **districts** called Herons' Home, Flowery Place, Sacred Precinct and Mosquito Fen.

SACRED PRECINCT

The Sacred Precinct was at the centre of the city. The Aztecs believed it was a holy place, and built huge temples there. Nearby stood the emperor's vast palace, surrounded by beautiful gardens and a noisy zoo. There were also sports courts for ball-games. Ordinary families lived around the outer edge of the city.

Giant stone statues stood at the foot of the steps leading up to the Great Temple in the Sacred Precinct.

MAKE A GREAT TEMPLE STATUE

The Aztecs carved huge stone statues to stand guard outside their temples. Make an Aztec statue to stand outside your room!

YOU WILL NEED:
BIG BOX • OLD PHONE BOOKS • STICKY TAPE • SPARE CARD • PENCIL • RULER • SHOE BOX • TWO MEDIUM BOXES • PAINT • BIG BRUSH • BLACK MARKER PEN

1

Fill the big box with old phone books to weigh it down. Tape it closed. Tape two medium boxes on top.

2

Draw a triangle on card. Ask an adult to cut it out. Tape the triangle to the shoe box as shown.

3

Tape the shoe box to the top of the column. Then paint the column with stone-coloured paint using a big brush.

4

Once it's dry, draw on the statue's face, arms, legs and loin cloth. Go over the lines with a black marker pen.

Your gigantic statue is sure to impress your friends and family! ▶

7

CHILLIES AND CHINAMPAS

Aztec farmers had to be inventive as Mesoamerica was not an easy place to grow food. The weather was extreme, especially on the mountains. Summers were baking hot, winters were cold and foggy, and rainfall was unreliable. The Aztecs' main crop was maize (sweetcorn). They planted it on mountain slopes and also on artificial islands called chinampas (say shee-nam-pah). These floating gardens were made of branches, with mud and stones on top. They were built beside the marshy shores of the lake.

The roots of trees growing on chinampas held the soil together. These farmers (front left) are using an Aztec digging-stick, called an uictli (say wheek-tlee).

COLOURFUL CROPS
On chinampas, farmers grew pumpkins, peppers, chillies, tomatoes, avocados, beans and peanuts. In a good year, they could produce seven harvests. The Aztec government controlled what was grown to make sure that there was a steady supply of food into the city.

A VARIED DIET
Aztec men hunted wild creatures for food, including deer, rabbits, ducks and geese. They used nets and hooks to catch fish from the lake. Boys searched for lizards, insects, grubs, worms, mushrooms and cactus leaves to eat. They also gathered blue-**algae** that grew on shallow water — it tasted like cheese. Hunters killed wild birds for their bright feathers and **jaguar** cats for their spotted skins.

DID YOU KNOW?
HUMAN POO MADE EXCELLENT MANURE TO HELP CROPS GROW. FARMERS COLLECTED THE POO FROM PUBLIC TOILETS IN HUTS BESIDE THE CANALS!

The rain-god Tlaloc (say Tlah-lock) was known as 'He Who Makes Things Grow'. The Aztecs worshipped him because without rain, there would be no crops.

8

MAKE A RAIN-GOD PENDANT

Aztec jewellery designs often featured gods. Make a pendant of Tlaloc, the god of rain and good harvests, in a few simple steps.

YOU WILL NEED:
AIR-DRYING CLAY • ROLLING PIN • TRACING PAPER • PENCIL • SCISSORS • MODELLING TOOL • ACRYLIC PAINTS • BRUSHES • STRING

1 Warm the clay in your hands for a few moments and then roll out a slab that's about 1cm thick.

2 Trace the image of Tlaloc from the page opposite. Cut your tracing out and place on the clay.

3 With a modelling tool, cut around your tracing. Cut zigzags along the top to make his crown.

4 Use a pencil to make two eye holes right through the clay. Add his nose, mouth and teeth.

5 When your pendant is dry, paint it in bright colours. Once the paint's dry, thread string through the eyes.

► Knot the string and wear!

9

FOOD AND SHELTER

Families ate two meals a day, at noon and in the evening. Ordinary people ate a mostly vegetarian diet as meat was very expensive. The food was simple. All meals were based on maize. It was crushed and stewed as porridge, or ground into flour and mixed with water to make dumplings and thin pancakes (today, called tortillas). Both were served with stewed vegetables, often spiced with hot chillies.

▲ Tortillas were cooked on a hot, flat stone over an open fire. The Aztecs ate with their fingers or scooped up food with tortillas.

▲ Maize flour was made from dried, ground-up maize (sweetcorn) grains.

DRINK AZTEC HOT CHOCOLATE

Sip the delicious chocolate drink that only important nobles were allowed to enjoy in Aztec times. Ask an adult to help!

YOU WILL NEED:
4 TBSP COCOA POWDER • 250 ML MILK • HONEY • VANILLA ESSENCE • HEATPROOF MEASURING JUG • SMALL SAUCEPAN • WHISK • MUG

1

Put the cocoa powder, a little of the milk, 1 tsp honey and a few vanilla drops in the jug. Stir.

3

Let the adult slowly pour the hot milk onto your cocoa mixture.

GIFTS FOR THE GODS

MOST AZTECS HAD A SMALL SHRINE TO THE GODS IN THEIR HOME. FAMILIES PUT OFFERINGS OF FOOD, FLOWERS OR DROPS OF BLOOD THERE, TO PLEASE THEIR GODS.

DRINKS

The Aztecs mainly drank water but on special occasions, beer made from cactus sap might be served. Rich people sometimes drank hot chocolate. This was made from rainforest cacao-tree beans, carried to Aztec lands by traders.

DID YOU KNOW?
IT WAS RUDE TO EAT OR DRINK TOO MUCH, AND DRUNKS WERE PUNISHED BY DEATH.

yndia mexicana

LIFE AT HOME

Most Aztec houses were small. They had one room with an open fire, a courtyard and a small bathroom. The fire was used for cooking and was never allowed to go out. House walls were built of dried mud bricks and the roofs were thatched with straw. Inside, there was not much furniture – Aztec people sat and slept on woven reed mats on the floor.

Aztecs made a chocolate drink by boiling crushed cacao beans in water. To make it frothy, they poured it from a great height.

2

Ask an adult to gently heat the rest of the milk in a saucepan until it is almost bubbling.

Let your hot chocolate cool down slightly before you enjoy drinking it!

4

Use a whisk to whip it up until it's frothy. Pour into a mug!

11

FAMILY LIFE

All Aztec families belonged to a **clan**, called a calpulli (say kal-pull-ee). Each calpulli organized its own affairs, from building schools to punishing members who broke the law. Within each family, men, women and children worked hard to support each other. Everyone had their own responsibilities. Men grew food, built houses and made useful things. Women cooked, wove cloth and cared for children and sick relatives.

Women used backstrap looms to weave cloth. The loom was tied to a post and a strap went around the weaver's waist.

From the age of six, children started to learn useful skills, such as hunting, weaving and house-cleaning, by watching and helping their parents. Aztec parents were strict. Boys and girls were expected to be obedient and respectful.

MATCHMAKING AND MARRIAGE

Grandparents passed on knowledge, experience and advice. Young people lived at home until they married, usually at the age of 20. Then they both lived with the boy's parents and worked for his family. Many marriages were arranged by old women who worked as **matchmakers**.

GOOD NEIGHBOURS

When there was a wedding, neighbours gathered for singing, dancing and a feast. But the Aztecs didn't need a special occasion to relax together. Aztec families lived close to one another and met to talk and play games, such as patolli.

DID YOU KNOW?

AT AN AZTEC WEDDING, THE BRIDE WAS CARRIED TO THE GROOM'S FAMILY HOUSE ON THE MATCHMAKER'S BACK.

A patolli board had 52 squares, one for each year in the Aztec 'century'. The Aztecs played to win, and some players bet everything they had on the result of the game.

PLAY PATOLLI

Try your hand at this exciting Aztec board game!

HOW TO PLAY

RULES FOR FOUR PLAYERS

Your aim is to get as many of your beans into the opposite player's base as you can. Take it in turns to roll the dice. When you throw a six, move onto your base and up the board. Roll again and move one counter at a time up the board. You can move forwards and sideways but not diagonally. If you land on a square with one of your opponent's beans already inside, it's yours. Whoever gets the most beans across the board without being captured, wins!

YOU WILL NEED:

42 x 42cm SQUARE THICK CARD
• RULER • PENCIL • FELT-TIP PEN.
• PAIR OF COMPASSES • PAINT AND BRUSHES OR FELT-TIP PENS • 6 MATCHING JELLY BEANS PER PLAYER • DICE

1

Mark the middle of each side of the square. In pencil, join up the marks to make a cross.

2

From the centre outwards, mark seven 2cm intervals along all four 'arms' of the cross.

3

Draw a line on either side of both 'arms' of the cross that is 2cm away from the crossed lines.

4

Use your marks to draw six lines across each 'arm'. Add semicircles at the ends. Go over the board in pen.

5

Set your compass to 4cm. Draw a circle in each corner of the board. Decorate in four different colours.

Keep your counters in your 'home zone' until you throw a six. Counters you've won from your opponent can also be kept in your home zone!

BASE

HOME ZONE

SCHOOL AND STUDY

At 14 years old, boys and girls had to go to school to learn to be good citizens. Most went to local classes called tepochalli (say teh-posh-kall-ee). They studied history and religion, traditional songs and simple counting. Boys also learned to march, obey orders, fight and handle weapons, ready to serve in the Aztec army.

Pupils arriving at a tepochalli. ▶

DID YOU KNOW?
EVERY 52 YEARS, THE FARMERS' CALENDAR AND THE HOLY CALENDAR ENDED ON THE SAME DAY. THIS MARKED THE END OF AN AZTEC 'CENTURY'.

SCHOOL DAYS
Boys from noble families went to high schools called calmecac (say kal-mesh-ak). They learned to be priests or government leaders. They studied law, and how to read and write Aztec picture-symbols. They also learned how to measure time, using the Aztecs' own special calendars

AZTEC CALENDARS
The Aztecs measured time in several different ways. Farmers used the sun calendar. It had 360 days, plus five extra. Priests and scribes used the holy calendar. It had 13 months, each with 20 days.

The 20 days of the holy calendar were named after creatures, everyday objects and powerful forces in the Aztec world.

▼

alligator   wind   house   lizard   serpent

death's head   water   rabbit   grass   dog

monkey   rain   reed   jaguar   vulture   eagle

movement   flint knife   deer   flower

MAKE AN AZTEC CALENDAR

Learn to measure time like an Aztec! Set the number **1** opposite the alligator. Then turn each wheel clockwise once a day to find the date's name and number.

YOU WILL NEED:
PAIR OF COMPASSES • 2 LARGE SHEETS OF WHITE CARD (ABOUT 50 x 20cm) • PENCIL • COLOURED FELT-TIP PENS OR PAINTS AND BRUSHES • 2 PAPER FASTENERS

1 Set the compass to 4cm and draw a circle on the card. Reset the compass to 10cm. Repeat. Cut the circles out.

2 Write 1–13 round the edge of the small circle. Copy or trace all the picture symbols onto the big circle.

3 On the other sheet of card, draw a line across the middle. Mark 7cm and then 22cm from the left edge.

4 Use a sharp pencil to make a hole in the centre of each circle and on the two marks on the card.

5 Use paper fasteners to fix the circles to the card. Write on 'Months', 'Days' and 'Today' as shown right.

Each day in the holy calendar had a name and a number. This was repeated only once each 260 days (the Aztec holy calendar year). Is it Two Lizard day today?

TODAY

MONTHS

DAYS

15

TREASURES!

The Aztecs were amazingly skilled craftworkers. They had no machines to help them, no strong iron tools and no potters' wheels. Using just their hands, and simple equipment, such as stone knives and wooden **mallets**, they made magnificent fans, masks, weapons, statues, jewels and stone-carvings. Craft skills were passed down from parents to children, and children started learning young.

Making a feather fan (left) and a feather headdress (right).

DIFFERENT DISTRICTS

Craftworkers lived and worked together in small communities. Different trades, such as goldsmiths or stonemasons, lived in particular areas of the city.

WEAR MOCTEZUMA'S HEADDRESS

Aztec rulers wore splendid headdresses made of priceless feathers and gold. Now you can wear one, too!

YOU WILL NEED:
PAIR OF COMPASSES • THIN CARD • PENCIL • RULER • SCISSORS • PAINT AND BRUSHES • GOLD GLITTER GLUE • GREEN, BLUE AND TURQUOISE PAPER • STICKY TAPE

1

Set your compass to 7.5cm. Draw a semicircle on card and cut it out. Cut out a smaller one in the centre.

This headdress probably belonged to the great Aztec ruler, Moctezuma (say Mock-th-zoh-mah).

4

Tape each of the feathers around the back of the mask. Try to alternate the colours.

16

FABULOUS FEATHERS

Feather-working was a traditional trade. The Aztecs got brightly coloured feathers from hunters who lived in the rainforests. The best feathers, from the blue-green **quetzal** bird, were more valuable than gold. Feather-workers turned them into fans and headdresses, and sewed them onto cloaks in elaborate patterns.

ONLY THE FINEST

Owning fine objects displayed **rank** and power. Only nobles and rulers were allowed to have the finest pottery, goldwork, fabric and fans. Sometimes the Aztecs asked other Mesoamericans, such as the Mixtecs who were master potters, to make goods for them.

Ask an adult or friend to help you tape the ends of the card strip together at the back. Now wear your headdress with pride, like an Aztec.

2

Paint on stripes of blue, green and brown for feathers. When dry, add dots of gold using glitter glue.

3

Make a feather template. Use it to draw and cut out 12 feathers from some blue and green paper.

5

Cut out a card strip long enough to go round your head with an overlap of 2cm. Glue headdress to the strip.

DID YOU KNOW?

OBSIDIAN, A GLASSY BLACK STONE, WAS USED BY TOP AZTEC CRAFTWORKERS TO MAKE MIRRORS AND RAZOR-SHARP ARROWHEADS. BUT OBSIDIAN WASN'T EASY TO FIND – IT WAS ONLY MADE BY EXPLODING VOLCANOES!

CLOTHES AND JEWELLERY

Clothes showed an Aztec's place in society. By law, ordinary people had to be simply dressed in plain, rough fabric made from cactus fibre. Only nobles were allowed softer cotton, patterned cloaks and eye-catching jewellery.

An Aztec nobleman and his wife in fine clothes. He wears a feather pendant; she has a necklace of shells. Both are wearing sandals with decorative laces.

Big, chunky necklaces and bracelets were made from gold.

FASHIONABLE CLOTHES
Most clothes were lengths of cloth that were wrapped around the body and tied in place. Women wore **tunics**, like ponchos, over long skirts. Men wore cloaks tied at the shoulder. Both men and women wore heavy, gold or **jade** jewellery – if they were rich enough. Some had pierced lips and ears. Among ordinary people, tattoos and body-paint were popular, cheap alternatives.

HAIR STYLES
Unmarried girls wore their hair loose. Married women plaited theirs and pinned the braids on the top of their head, like horns. Boys had long hair until they had captured an enemy in battle. Only then were they allowed to cut their hair to shoulder length, like grown men.

Only nobles, or soldiers whose legs had been badly scarred in battle, were allowed to wear cloaks that reached below their knees.

18

MAKE AN AZTEC NOBLE'S CLOAK

Your Aztec cloak will remind everyone that you're a very important person. Remember to put on your ankle ornaments, too!

YOU WILL NEED:
WHITE FABRIC (90 x 120cm)
• POSTER OR FABRIC PAINTS
• BRUSHES • PENCIL • 150cm
LENGTH OF RIBBON • SCISSORS
• GLUE • PAIR OF COMPASSES
• YELLOW CARD • 2 x 20cm
LENGTHS OF WHITE RIBBON

1

Draw a margin around the edge of the material then another line inside it. Add circles around the edge.

2

Paint the inner margin red and the gaps between the circles blue. Add blue criss-crosses.

3

Paint a red dot inside each circle. Once the paint's dry, glue ribbon along one short edge. Allow extra at each end.

Put on your cloak and tie the ribbons. Tie the card strips around your ankles – now you look like a real Aztec!

4

Cut out eight circles from yellow card. Glue four circles, evenly spaced, along each of your ribbon strips.

AT THE MARKET

All Aztec towns and cities had a marketplace. Merchants, craftworkers and farmers met there, to **barter** (exchange) goods. Aztecs did not have coins, instead they used valuable items such as cacao beans or feathers as money.

Buyers and sellers hoped to get a good deal at the market.

BUSTLING MARKET
Most market traders were women. They set up stalls to sell goods produced by their families, such as vegetables, flowers, cloth, mats and pots. Foreign traders brought gold dust and sea-shells from the coast, or animal skins and feathers from the rainforest. Government officials also sold valuable goods that they had claimed as tribute (tax) from people they had conquered.

TLATELOLCO CITY
In 1473 CE the Aztecs conquered the nearby city of Tlatelolco (say Tlah-teh-loll-coh) and it became the greatest trading place in Mesoamerica. The Aztecs had no wheeled transport or horses. Porters and merchants carried goods on their backs for hundreds of miles. Merchants travelled so much and met so many different people, that Aztec rulers sometimes used them as spies.

Aztec traders brought this monkey pot from the city of Texcoco to sell. It is carved from shiny black obsidian (stone produced by erupting volcanoes).

MAKE A MONKEY POT

Make a clay pot using the same coil technique as the Aztecs. Ozomatli (say Oh-zoh-maht-lee), the Monkey-god, protected art, games and fun.

1 Shape the clay into balls. Then use your hands to roll out the balls into several long thin 'sausages'.

2 Fold in one end of the first sausage and then coil the rest round and round to build up the pot.

3 If you need to add another sausage, just blend the end on. When the pot is big enough, smooth the sides.

4 Roll a 10p-sized ball of clay for the head and four small sausages for the feet. Shape the head and feet.

5 Attach the head and feet to the pot and smooth the joins. When the clay has dried out, paint it black.

To make your pot shine, use a clean brush to add a layer of PVA mixture (mix three parts PVA to one part water). ▶

READY FOR WAR

The Aztecs were always ready for war and had a well-organized army. They attacked and conquered neighbouring countries, took their land and then demanded tribute (tax) from them. They also took people captive and made them slaves.

Warriors tried to capture enemies alive so that priests could kill them later, as **sacrifices**.

SHOWING COURAGE

Aztec people admired warriors. Young men had to join the army at the age of 17. To show his strength, each ruler had to start his **reign** with a battle. The Aztecs believed it was better to live a short, brave life and die in battle, than **surrender** or retreat. Top warriors were called eagle or jaguar knights.

DRESS UP AS AN AZTEC WARRIOR

Warriors wore real jaguar skins to show that they shared the strength and fierceness of a big cat. Make a frightening, fake jaguar skin.

YOU WILL NEED:
1 x 1m WHITE COTTON FABRIC • SEWING SCISSORS • PENCIL • BLACK MARKER PEN • ACRYLIC OR POSTER PAINTS • BRUSHES • 2 x 40cm LENGTHS OF RED RIBBON

1

Fold the fabric diagonally to make a large triangle. Now cut along the fold.

Put on your jaguar cloak and feel strong and brave, just like an Aztec warrior.

WEAPONS AND ARMOUR

Aztec warriors were armed with wooden spears and war-clubs tipped with razor-sharp flakes of **flint**. Their armour was made of quilted cotton soaked in salty water, and this made it surprisingly tough and strong. For extra protection, warriors carried round wood or leather shields: the finest were trimmed with fur or feathers.

Aztec warriors carrying a shield (left) and bag full of arrows (right) made of spotted jaguar skin.

In pencil, draw on the body, tail, front legs and head. Draw dots all over your jaguar's body.

With a black marker pen, carefully go over all your pencil lines so the jaguar's features really stand out.

Mix up orange paint and colour in the jaguar. Don't go over the black lines! Add the spots with black pen.

With scissors, snip a tiny hole on each side of the jaguar's head. Thread red ribbon through each of the holes.

The Aztecs thought that gods controlled everything in the universe including the sun, wind, rain, growing crops, families, travellers, death, disease and war. They believed that their leader was **descended** from a god. The Aztecs built stepped pyramids with temples at the top. These mountain-like buildings were designed to rise above the earth so the Aztecs were closer to the gods.

No Aztec pyramid temples have survived. But they would have looked like this pyramid, built by earlier Mexican people in the city of Teotihuacan.

DID YOU KNOW?

AN ORDINARY PERSON WISHING TO SPEAK TO A RULER AT THE PALACE, HAD TO KEEP THEIR EYES LOOKING DOWN AND BOW VERY LOW. WHEN THEY LEFT, THEY WALKED BACKWARDS AS IT WAS VERY RUDE TO FACE AWAY FROM THE RULER.

RULERS AND GOVERNMENT

The leader of the Aztecs was called the Speaker and his deputy was the Snake-woman. They were all-powerful. The Speaker made laws and was head of the army. The Snake-woman ran the government. At the start of the Aztec civilization, rulers were chosen from the best warriors. Eventually this changed and they were chosen only from the last ruler's family.

This mask is of the god Tezcatlipoca (say Tess-kah-tlee-poh-ka). It is a real skull covered in a mosaic of semi-precious stones.

LAW AND ORDER

Rulers were surrounded by a **ruling class** of well-trained officials, priests, noblemen, judges and scribes. But most Aztecs were poor, ordinary folk known as 'macehuatlin' (say mah-shee-wat-lin). Below them came slaves who were prisoners-of-war, criminals or very poor. Ordinary peoples' lives were strictly controlled by tough Aztec laws and harsh punishments. The penalty for many crimes was death, beating or torture.

MAKE AN AZTEC MASK

This death mask is guaranteed to frighten your friends. Tezcatlipoca was the god of night and the future. Aztecs believed he started wars.

YOU WILL NEED:
THIN BLACK CARD ABOUT 25 x 25cm • RULER • PENCIL • SCISSORS • CRAFT KNIFE • SILVER FOIL • BLUE, GREEN, TURQUOISE, BLACK AND WHITE PAPER • GLUE • ELASTIC THREAD • WHITE FELT OR CARD

1

Measure your face. Draw an oval shape on the card that's big enough to cover your face completely.

2

Draw on the eyes, mouth and nose. Then ask an adult to cut them out with a craft knife.

3

Glue on two wide strips of foil. Cut out the eye, nose and mouth holes. Glue on coloured paper shapes.

4

Use a sharp pencil to make holes for the elastic at each side of the mask, below the eyes.

5

Finally, thread elastic through the side holes. Put the mask on. Gently tighten the elastic and knot to secure.

Put on your mask and imagine that you can see into the future, like a god.

CEREMONIES AND SACRIFICES

Religious ceremonies were an essential part of Aztec life. They linked people to the mighty gods. The Aztecs **worshipped** by saying prayers, singing, dancing and offering flowers, incense and gold.

In the game 'volador', four men tied to ropes jumped from a tall pole. They tried to fly round, like the sun moving across the sky. They aimed to make 52 turns, one for each year in an Aztec century.

THE LAST WORLD

Aztecs thought that the world had been created, then destroyed, four times before. They were living in the fifth world – and it was the final one! To stop their world coming to an end, Aztec men and women 'fed' the gods with life-giving blood. They pricked their ear-lobes every day, to produce two drops as an offering. At holy festivals, they sacrificed hundreds of humans, mostly war-captives, to the gods.

DON'T TRY THIS AT HOME

HUMAN SACRIFICE

The ideal sacrifice was male, young, brave, strong and handsome. In Aztec eyes, this was the most valuable kind of person. Aztec priests killed victims at the top of temple steps, by cutting out their hearts and letting their blood flow down. Aztec sports also had a religious purpose, to help keep the world alive. Winners were often sacrificed!

Aztec musicians play a leather-topped drum (left) and a hollow wooden drum (centre) while dancers shake rattles and wave fans.

MAKE AN AZTEC RATTLE

Whistles, rattles and drums were played by musicians at ceremonies. Make your own rattle and have a go!

YOU WILL NEED:
BALLOON • PETROLEUM JELLY • NEWSPAPER • PVA MIXTURE (3 PARTS PVA TO ONE PART WATER) • BOWL • SCISSORS • THIN DOWEL ROD • RAW SEEDS OR LENTILS • MASKING TAPE • ACRYLIC PAINTS • BRUSHES • SMALL FEATHERS

1 Blow up your balloon and cover in jelly. Dip strips of newspaper in the PVA mixture and cover the balloon.

2 When dry, pop the balloon and remove it. Carefully pour raw lentils in through the hole.

3 Push the rod into the rattle. Keep it upright and put lots of small strips of masking tape around hole and rod.

4 Paint your rattle brown. When the paint's dry, add zigzags and dots. Then tape two feathers to the top.

▲ Shake your rattle while your friend taps out a rhythm on a table top!

THE END OF THE WORLD?

In spite of making sacrifices to their gods, the Aztecs were still fearful. Ancient legends told how the snake-god Quetzalcoatl would arrive and bring the world to an end. The Aztecs expected to see strange signs before he arrived and, in 1519 CE, this seemed to be happening. Aztec ruler Moctezuma had nightmares about the future. Priests saw **eclipses** of the sun and a blazing **comet**. Monstrous four-legged men were reported.

At first, the Aztecs greeted Europeans peacefully. They did not realize that the Europeans wanted their land.

MAKE A FOLDING CODEX

The Aztecs recorded their history by writing with picture symbols in folding books called codexes. Find out how to make your own.

YOU WILL NEED:
LARGE SHEET OF THIN WHITE CARD • RULER • PENCIL • COLOURED PENCILS

1

Cut a 125 x 25cm strip of card. Measure, mark and then draw four lines on the strip, 25cm apart.

3

Starting at the back, in the top right-hand corner, draw picture symbols (see p29) into the codex.

Historians have learned a lot about Aztec life by reading codexes that have survived. The Aztecs started writing at the back of each codex, in the top right-hand corner.

THE SPANISH ARRIVE

In fact, a Spanish explorer named Hernan Cortes had landed on the Mesoamerican coast. He came in search of treasure. The 'monsters' were his men riding horses; the Aztecs had never seen them before. Cortes and his men marched towards Tenochtitlan, helped by the Aztecs' enemies. Many peoples that the Aztecs had conquered now wanted to see them destroyed.

THE END OF THE AZTECS

In 1520 CE, the Aztecs drove Cortes away, but Moctezuma was killed. The next year, Cortes returned. He destroyed the city and killed most of its citizens. Within 100 years, European diseases that the Spanish brought with them had almost wiped out the Aztec people and their fascinating civilization.

DID YOU KNOW?

CODEX PAINTERS WERE HIGHLY THOUGHT OF AND KNOWN AS TLACUILO (SAY TLAH-KHWEE-LOH) WHICH MEANS 'PUTTER DOWN OF THOUGHTS'.

2

Line your ruler up with the first line and make a fold. Use this method to fold the strip into a concertina.

You could design your own picture symbols showing some of the things you do and see every day. ▶

4

Colour in your picture symbols using coloured pencils. You could go over them in black felt-tip pen, too.

algae Simple life-forms, related to animals, plants and bacteria. Often they appear as slime or seaweed.

aqueduct A high bridge specially designed to carry water over land.

barter Exchange goods for others of equal value.

causeway Road raised above the surrounding ground on a mound of earth or stones.

clan Group of families that share the same ancestors.

comet A ball of ice and dust, travelling though space.

descended To be related to your ancestors. You are descended from your parents and grandparents.

districts Specific areas within a big city or large area of countryside

dominated Ruled over or controlled by.

eclipse (solar) When the Moon passes in front of the sun, blocking out its light.

flint A hard rock that can be made into a sharp cutting edge.

jade A pale green, shiny and hard precious stone.

jaguar Large, fierce wild cat with spotted skin.

mallet Wooden hammer.

matchmaker Person who finds partners for single people to marry.

Maya Mesoamerican people who built cities in the rainforests. Most powerful between 300 – 900 CE.

quetzal Rainforest bird with beautiful green feathers.

rank A person's place in society.

reign Length of time that a ruler stays in power.

ruling class Powerful group in a society that controls other people in the same society.

sacrifice Killing people or animals to please the gods.

surrender Give up and hand over power.

Toltec Mesoamerican people who ruled the Central Valley of Mexico from around 900 – 1200 CE.

tunic Long, straight piece of clothing with no sleeves.

worship To respect, love or fear a god or goddess.

INDEX

NOTES FOR PARENTS AND TEACHERS

• The Aztecs loved music and dancing. The children can listen to the sound of Aztec music on http://www.princetonartmuseum.org/Jaguar/jaguar.html and http://www.mexicolore.co.uk/index.php?one=azt&two=mus. Encourage the children to copy some Aztec sounds and rhythms on drums, recorders or any other instruments that they can play.

• The Aztecs believed that they could see a giant rabbit on the surface of the moon. Take your child outside one dark night when the moon is full. You can find a picture of the rabbit, and read an Aztec legend about the Moon at http://www.adlerplanetarium.org/cyberspace/moon/culture.html. Do not allow your child to go out at night unaccompanied.

• Research some Aztec stories. For example, Star Snake is the hero of an exciting story written by Martin Auer, from Austria, in 2000. You can find Star Snake's story online at http://www.mexconnect.com/mex_/travel/kmetzger/kmstarsnake.html. Read this, or another story, to the children. Ask them to first imagine themselves as Aztecs and then to write their own story.

• Many Aztec customs still survive today. Every year, on 31st October, Mexicans celebrate the Day of the Dead to honour their dead ancestors. Families decorate tombs, hold feasts, join in processions, make skeleton dolls and eat sweets shaped like skulls! Help the children to make a papier-mâché piñata or skeleton dolls.

• With the children, create an enormous Aztec timeline frieze. Research important events in Aztec history in the library or on the internet (see http://www.metmuseum.org/toah/ht/08/canm/ht08canm.htm). Mark on the events and ask the children to draw and colour pictures for each significant date.

• The Aztecs used picture symbols for writing numbers, as well as words. Look for reference material on Aztec numbers at the library or on the internet (try http://www.ancientscripts.com/aztec.html). Create a simple 'code book' of numbers and symbols, and photocopy one for each of the children. Then create picture sums or simple games for the children – or ask them to 'write' their birthday date in picture symbols.

Useful websites
Mexicolore is an excellent resource for the study of Mexico and the Aztecs, compiled by teachers and entertainers. http://www.mexicolore.co.uk/index.php.

Children can play Aztec games at: http://www.mesoweb.com/crystal/index.html#.

Visit the website of a museum near the ruins of the Great Temple in what was Tenochtitlan: http://archaeology.la.asu.edu/tm/index2.php